LEANING POST
for Children Too

Lilieth Dorman

Leaning Post for Children Too

Copyright © 2023 by Lilieth Dorman. All rights reserved.

No part of this publication may be reproduced, stored in a retrieval system or transmitted in any way by any means, electronic, mechanical, photocopy, recording or otherwise without the prior permission of the author except as provided by USA copyright law.

The opinions expressed by the author are not necessarily those of URLink Print and Media.

1603 Capitol Ave., Suite 310 Cheyenne, Wyoming USA 82001
1-888-980-6523 | admin@urlinkpublishing.com

URLink Print and Media is committed to excellence in the publishing industry.

Book design copyright © 2023 by URLink Print and Media. All rights reserved.

Published in the United States of America

Library of Congress Control Number: 2023904476
ISBN 978-1-68486-389-1 (Paperback)
ISBN 978-1-68486-390-7 (Digital)

01.03.2023

To Apostle Juliet. Thanks for all your love and prayers. Your continued encouragement and push to become all that God desires. You are an example of humility that affects every person that you encounter. Your love for people all around is contagious and inspiring. The children you have are more than you birthed and there is love for all. Blessings.

Thank you God for helping me to do the right things.
Thank you for my family and my friends.

Rayne Cooper

Hear the children pray
Not what we would say
But what is in their heart.
As words flow, from them freely,
They come to know him as their savior too
A friend to them he is true.

A prayer they will pray
That only a child can say.
Listen to them worship our King
As only children can bring.
I found that our savior is
And always will be,
Just as close to them
As he is to you me.

The words flow smooth
Nothing they have to prove
Because little ones do not have hidden
In their hearts weighty treasures to remove
They see through untainted eyes
The world as God paints not lies.

Yes children can run to him
There is no stopping his love for them
His arms are wide open to receive
Every child and every need,
Family matters, friends gone wrong;
For all their cares, he shows up strong.

He has placed within each child
A precious heart so meek and mild.
And as we teach them when they grow
Their love for him they will surely show.
Each heart to shine so bright
As God fills them with his light.

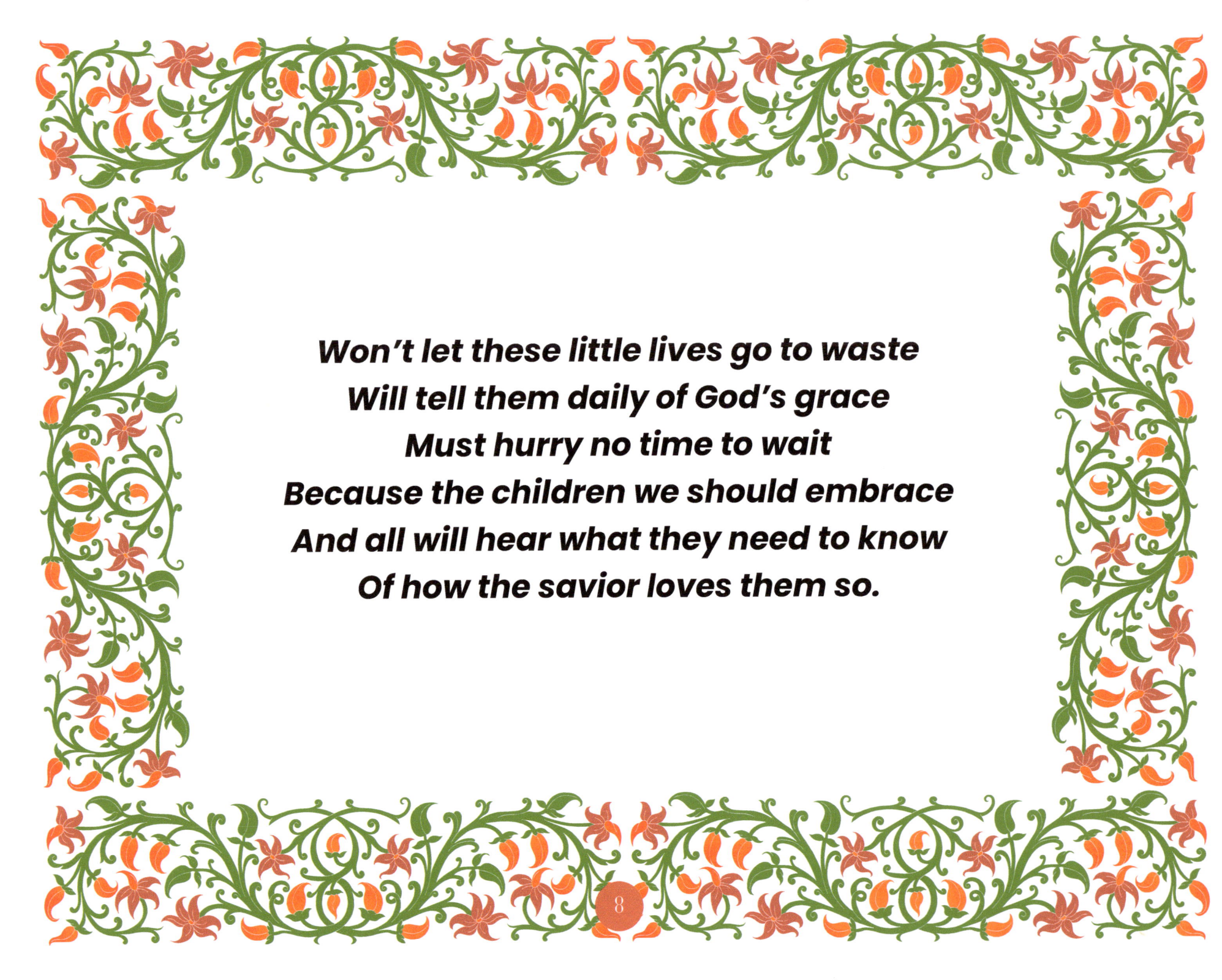

Won't let these little lives go to waste
Will tell them daily of God's grace
Must hurry no time to wait
Because the children we should embrace
And all will hear what they need to know
Of how the savior loves them so.

There is a song that we can sing
Then children too will let it ring
A daily song to show them now
The savior cares and here is how
The words are true for all who do
Please share now, I will, won't you.

Songs:-

Jesus loves me this I know
For the Bible tells me so
Little ones to him belong
They are weak but he is strong

Yes, Jesus loves me
Yes, Jesus loves me
Yes Jesus loves me
The Bible tells me so.

The B-I-B-L-E
That's the book for me
I stand alone on the word of God
The B-I-B-L-E

*Now show us how to keep each one safe
As we teach them how to seek your face,
So each can come to know the most
When they turn to the leaning post.*

Deuteronomy 6:6-7a

"And these words, which I command thee this day, shall be in thine heart: And thou shalt teach them diligently unto thy children, Amen.

www.ingramcontent.com/pod-product-compliance
Lightning Source LLC
LaVergne TN
LVHW071733060526
838200LV00031B/487